About the Author

Kaitlyn is passionate about the written word and doesn't think that anyone is too young to learn new words and discover the joy of reading. With a strong love for family and animals, she enjoys teaching her children about their animal friends and making up stories of their adventures as they live out their lives on their farm in central Alberta.

To my husband for always supporting me and to
my children for helping me to create these
stories.

Coming soon :
Kittens in the Barn
Bunnies in the Meadow

AT PATCHWORK FARMS UP BY THE HOUSE,

YOU WILL FIND HIM BARKING AT

EVERY LITTLE MOUSE!

HE IS BIG AND LOUD,

BUT HE IS NOT MEAN.

HE IS MY BIG LOVABLE

PUPPY, NO NEED TO

SCREAM.

HIS NAME IS DOC AND HE LOVES
TO PLAY FETCH!
TO SAY IT'S HIS FAVORITE THING
IS NOT ...

...A STRETCH.

HE WILL RUN AND RUN ALL DAY

AND NIGHT.

YOU SHOULD SEE HIM JUMP, IT IS QUITE A SIGHT!

HE IS BIG AND YELLOW
AND A GREAT BIG GOOF.

IF YOU TELL HIM TO
SPEAK HE WILL SAY

WOOF!
DOC

I LOVE HIM SO MUCH!

HE IS MY SILLY OLD MAN.

I'M HIS LITTLE GIRL AND HE IS MY BIGGEST FAN!

Doc The Dog
Patchwork Farm